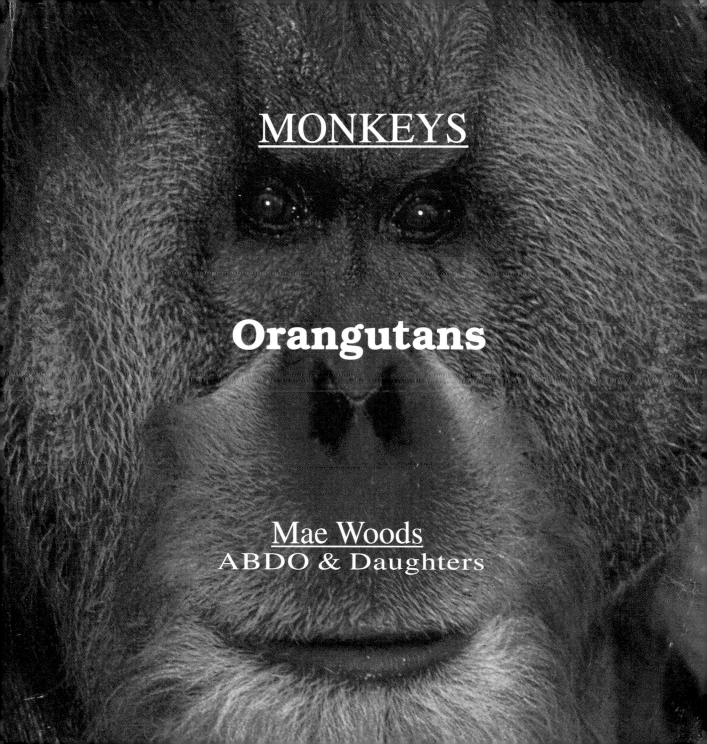

MONKEYS

Orangutans

Mae Woods
ABDO & Daughters

visit us at
www.abdopub.com

Published by Abdo & Daughters, 4940 Viking Drive, Suite 622, Edina, Minnesota 55435.

Copyright © 1998 by Abdo Consulting Group, Inc., Pentagon Tower, P.O. Box 36036, Minneapolis, Minnesota 55435 USA. International copyrights reserved in all countries. No part of this book may be reproduced in any form without written permission from the publisher.

Printed in the United States.

Cover Photo credits: Peter Arnold, Inc.
Interior Photo credits: Peter Arnold, Inc.

Edited by Lori Kinstad Pupeza

Library of Congress Cataloging-in-Publication Data

Woods, Mae.
     Orangutans / Mae Woods.
     p. cm. -- (Monkeys)
     Includes index.
     Summary: Describes the physical appearance and the behavior of the ape with the long red hair and the long arms that nearly touch the ground.
     ISBN 1-56239-600-5
     1. Orangutan--Juvenile literature. [1. Orangutan.] I. Title. II. Series: Woods, Mae. Monkeys.
     QL737.P96W65   1998
     599.88'42--dc20

                                    96-313
                                    CIP
                                    AC

Contents

Orangutans And Other Primates

Apes, monkeys, and humans are **primates**. Orangutans are in the family of great apes along with **gorillas** and **chimpanzees**. The word orangutan means "person of the forest." They are sometimes called red apes because their bodies are covered with long reddish hair. Apes and monkeys live for 35 to 40 years.

In many ways they are like people. Primates share many physical **traits**. They are able to use their hands to grasp objects. This allows them to do many things other animals cannot. They can gather food. They can carry objects. They can build things.

Orangutans are often called red apes because of their hair color.

Orangutan Features

Orangutans feel emotions just like humans do. They express their feelings by making sounds and facial movements. People have **vocal chords** that allow them to speak. Apes do not. But apes living in **captivity** have been able to learn **sign language** to **communicate** with humans.

Each orangutan is **unique** in appearance. Each one looks different and has a distinct **personality**.

Opposite page: Orangutans express emotion through facial expressions.

Adult Orangutans

As orangutans grow their bodies change. An adult male orangutan has a beard and wide, hairless cheeks. He develops a pouch of skin around his throat that makes his voice deep and loud. He roars in the morning and at night. This **long call** tells other animals where he is and keeps them away.

Adult male orangutans grow to a height of 4 1/2 feet (1.4 m) and may weigh up to 200 pounds (91 kg). When they are full grown it becomes difficult for them to climb trees. They may break the branches and fall. Older animals spend more time on the ground than in the trees.

Females are smaller. They weigh about 90 pounds (41 kg) and are about 4 feet tall (1.2 m). A small orangutan is the height of a six year old human.

This adult Orangutan has a beard and wide cheeks.

Where They Live

Orangutans are found in Indonesia on the islands of Borneo and Sumatra. They live in tropical rain forests where trees and water are **plentiful**.

Each evening they build nests out of leaves and branches and sleep in the tree tops. If it is raining they also make a leafy roof to keep from getting too wet. They like to move from place to place, so the next night they will pick a new spot for their sleeping nest.

Orangutans are **solitary**. Mothers and babies always live together, but other orangutans sleep in separate nests and go out alone to hunt for food.

Detail area

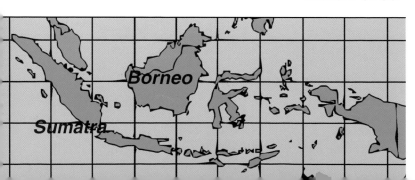

An Orangutan building a nest in Borneo.

Food

Orangutans have such large **appetites** that they may spend the entire day searching for food and eating. They eat fruits, vegetables, leaves, flowers, nuts, bark, insects, and eggs.

They have sharp teeth in the front for cutting and tearing food and **molars** in the back for chewing.

Orangutans are very smart. They know that each type of tree bears fruit at different times of the year. As the **seasons** change, the animals remember the locations of all the trees that may have ripe fruit. That's where they will go that day.

The insects they like to eat are **termites** and ants. When they find an ant hill or a termite nest, they poke a stick into it. The insects climb up the stick. Then the clever orangutans pull it out and lick them off. After orangutans eat, they like to take a nap.

An orangutan eating leaves and bark.

Babies

Mothers keep their babies close to them until they are four or five years old. Usually, the babies ride on their mothers' backs. They also share their mothers' sleeping nests at night.

Mothers **groom** their babies. She picks through her baby's hair, picking out dirt or insects and smoothing out the tangles. Young orangutans enjoy this and learn it is a gesture of friendship and good will. When they grow older, they will groom their mothers and their friends.

Opposite page: Orangutan mother and young.

Young Orangutans

Young orangutans need to be taught to travel by swinging from tree to tree. When they are up high, they are safe from other animals on the ground. Their mothers show them how to hook their fingers over a branch, swing forward, and grasp another one. Mothers will not leave their babies until they have learned this skill.

Opposite page: A young orangutan swinging from a tree.

Glossary

agile (AJ-ahl) - Able to move quickly and easily.

appetite (AP-a-tite) - The desire to eat.

captivity (cap-TIV-it-e) - Being held in one place, such as a zoo.

chimpanzees - A group of small, dark-haired apes from Africa.

communicate (kuh-mew-nih-KATE) - To express thoughts and ideas.

gorillas - A group of large African apes with thick bodies and dark hair.

groom - To clean and care for.

long call - A vocal sound made by adult male orangutans.

molars - Teeth with a flat surface in the back of the mouth.

personality (pur-sah-NAL-i-tee) - All the traits that make one person different from another.

plentiful - A large amount.

primates (PRIE-maytes) - A group of animals that includes humans, apes, and monkeys.

seasons - Different times of the year: spring, summer, autumn, and winter.

sign language - A system of hand gestures used to express ideas.

solitary (SAL e tar e) - Being or living alone.

termites - Small burrowing insects that eat wood.

trait (TRAY-t) - Qualities that help set apart one thing from another.

unique (yoo-NEEK) - One of a kind.

vocal chords - The body part that enables humans to speak.

Index